SCARFE ON STAGE

To Jane

HAMISH HAMILTON LTD

Published by the Penguin Group
Penguin Books Ltd, 27 Wrights Lane, London W8 5TZ, England
Penguin Books USA Inc., 375 Hudson Street, New York, New York 10014, USA
Penguin Books Australia Ltd, Ringwood, Victoria, Australia
Penguin Books Canada Ltd, 10 Alcorn Avenue, Toronto, Ontario, Canada M4V 3B2
Penguin Books (NZ) Ltd, 182–190 Wairau Road, Auckland 10, New Zealand

Penguin Books Ltd, Registered Offices: Harmondsworth, Middlesex, England

First Published in Great Britain by Hamish Hamilton Ltd 1992
1 3 5 7 9 10 8 6 4 2

Copyright © Gerald Scarfe, 1992
The moral right of the author has been asserted

A CIP catalogue record for this book is available from the British Library
ISBN 0-241-131871

Photographs are reproduced by courtesy of:
Brian Harris/ The Independent (Pink Floyd The Wall in Berlin), Radio Times (Scarfe
by Scarfe), Radio Times and Sally George (I Like the Girls Who Do ...), John
Green/Noel Gay Television (Ten Glorious Years), Vanessa Courtney (Scarfe's
Follies), Zoë Dominic (Orpheus in the Underworld).
Back jacket photograph by Mark Bourdillon.

SCARFE ON STAGE

HAMISH HAMILTON · LONDON

Peter Hall rehearses David Warner in *Hamlet*. Sketched
from life in Stratford-upon-Avon, 1964

INTRODUCTION
by Sir Peter Hall

Good stage design is like a mask. It must of course be beautiful in itself, but it must remain ambiguous enough to let the meaning of the play come through. Stage design is a delicate activity because it must not do all the work of the playwright: it should support what he means, not pre-empt it. It follows, therefore, that a great artist is sometimes not necessarily a great stage designer, for he may say too much. Dali's *Salome* was very beautiful but there was not much for the opera to say. A fine mask has grace, proportion and neutrality – so that it appears to cry when the action is sad, or laugh when the action is comic. A good set must do the same.

Gerald Scarfe is a great stage designer – yet you could hardly call his talent neutral or ambiguous. He is, of course, a superb draughtsman in the English tradition. He has a line which is graceful, witty and eloquent. But underneath the humour, you always sense his ferocious dislike of stupidity, hypocrisy and rapaciousness – particularly the rapaciousness which demands power. Sometimes his indictments make up a bestiary, in which the men and women who are his targets are the beast. But these beasts fight for domination, not survival. Like all great satirists, Gerald Scarfe is an idealist. If he didn't believe strongly, he would not castigate so passionately.

As a friend or as a fellow-worker in the theatre, he is wise, witty and gentle. But encouraged by the licence of ink, he can be a terrible scourge – particularly of public characters who pretend to be what they are not.

All this puts him among the great English satirists, and hardly, one would have thought, fits him for the stage. But his art has grace, a wonderful sense of colour, and a paradoxical ability to make ugly images quite beautiful. He takes reality and distorts it, but ends up with an image which is surreal – more real than reality, and therefore very potent in the theatre.

If you examine Gerald Scarfe's work in theatre, opera and film, the paradox of his gentle yet ferocious character becomes more evident. There is a succession of strong designs, expressing an extreme reaction to the work he is setting. There is apparently not much room here for ambiguity or for neutrality. He responds in quite a primitive way to the playwright or to the composer and makes a vivid comment.

But stage design can, again like the mask, deal with the grotesque and the extreme. And this will work *providing* that what the set is heightening truly belongs at the heart of the play. It must not be a distortion or a simplification. Done with honesty, the vivid comment supports the meaning of the play and neither limits nor denies it.

Gerald Scarfe makes the theatre surreal again. This is the achievement of his work in the performing arts. The bland naturalism of most film and television design has released the theatre from naturalistic obligations and allowed it to go back to its origins. It is once more a place of fantasy and dreams. The audience always know that they are in a theatre, and they always know that they are playing a game of make-believe. So the surreal, the expressionistic, and the unexpected are coming back

to the theatre and bringing poetry with them. This
is not only the poetry of words, but the poetry of
actions, of emblems, of colour and design.

'Theatricality' is now unfortunately a pejorative
word. We need a new word for the poetic essence
of theatre – its very *theatreness*. Gerald Scarfe is
part of this tendency because he takes a play or an
opera and gives it a surreal strength. At his best, he
makes an audience understand by the very vividness
of his images. And he makes them understand not
just his reaction to the play, but the play itself.

Right: Poster advertising the album *Pink Floyd The Wall*, 1979, showing the praying-mantis-like Wife

Overleaf: Design for live-action sequence in *Pink Floyd The Wall*: the Wife's shadow menaces Pink

PINK FLOYD

THE WALL

Gerald Scarfe

Their new double album

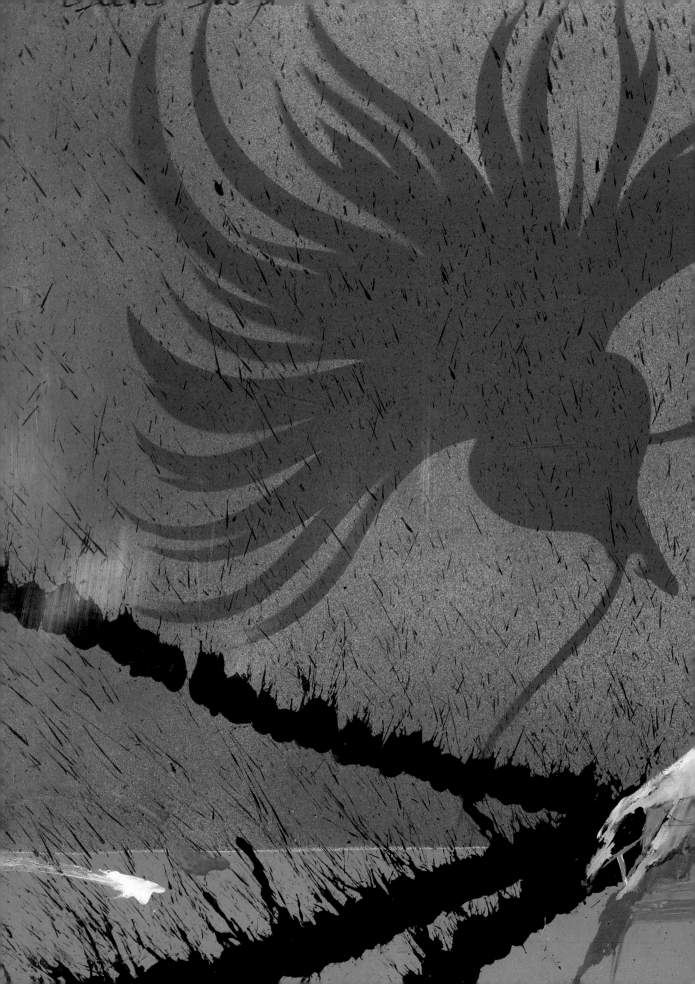

Animation stills from 'Goodbye Blue Skies', *Pink Floyd The Wall.*
Above: The Eagle of War swoops to conquer
Below: The Frightened Ones run for cover during the Blitz

Right: The Warlord rises above the City
Lower right: The Warlord turns to metal and sends out squadrons of bombers
Overleaf: The Marching Hammers

An Alan Parker Film
Pink Floyd
The Wall
by Roger Waters
Designed by Gerald Scarfe
With Bob Geldof as Pink
Film Music Produced by Roger Waters and David Gilmour
Executive Producer Steve O'Rourke
Produced by Alan Marshall
Animation Directed by Gerald Scarfe
Screenplay by Roger Waters
Directed by Alan Parker
© 1982 Metro-Goldwyn-Mayer Film Co. and SLM Entertainment Ltd.
Distributed by
MGM/UA
Entertainment Co.

Above: Live-action 'Education' sequence from the film
Below: Original design for this sequence showing the processing of children carried slowly forward on a conveyor belt

Left: Poster for the film

Overleaf: The Flowers meet, mate and die. Animation sequence from the film

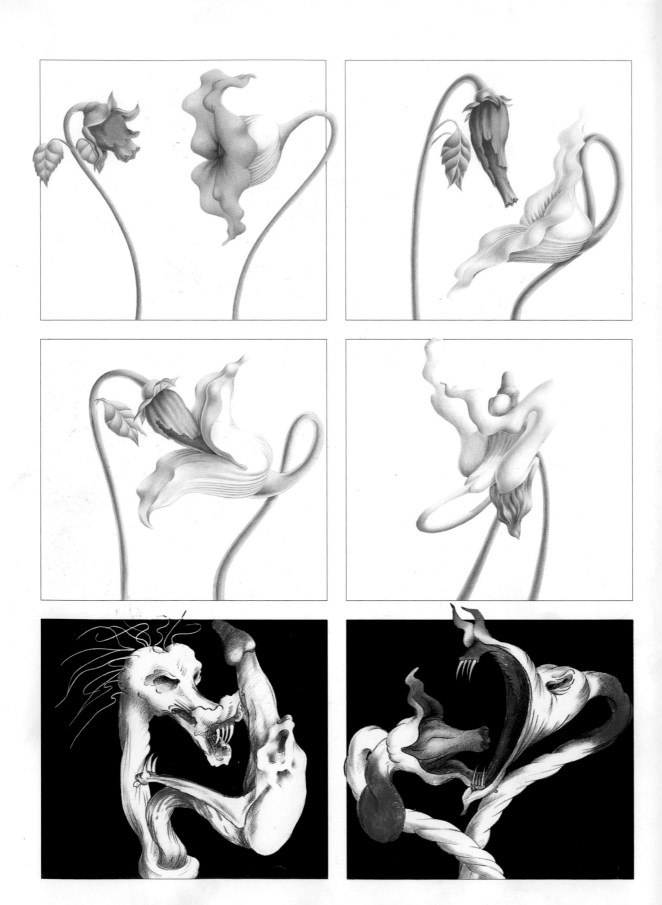

Poster for *Who's a Lucky Boy?*, Manchester Royal Exchange, 1985

Left: Costume designs for *Who's a Lucky Boy?*
Depressed Housewife and Punk Businessman

Above: Set design for *Who's a Lucky Boy?*, a musical
based on Hogarth's *The Rake's Progress*. The
Unemployed enter the drain

The Hero is trapped inside the skull

The Commander-in-Chief

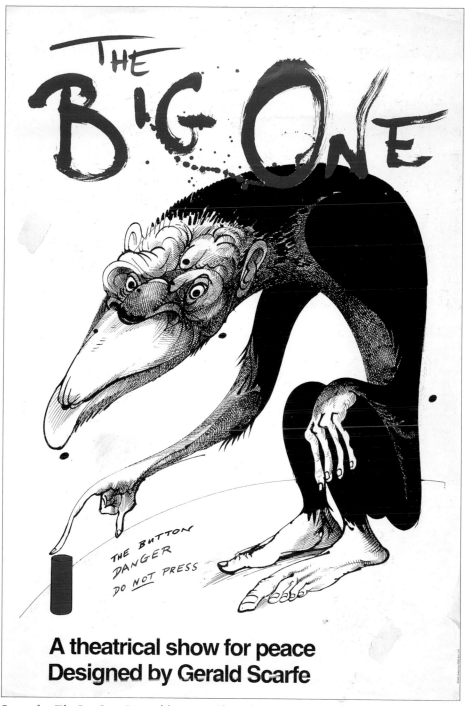

Poster for *The Big One*. Devised by Susannah York and
Bill Bachle. Dominion Theatre, 1983

Overleaf: 'In the Beginning', Part Two. Backcloth
design for *The Big One*

Poster design for *Serious Money*, Royal Court Theatre, 1987

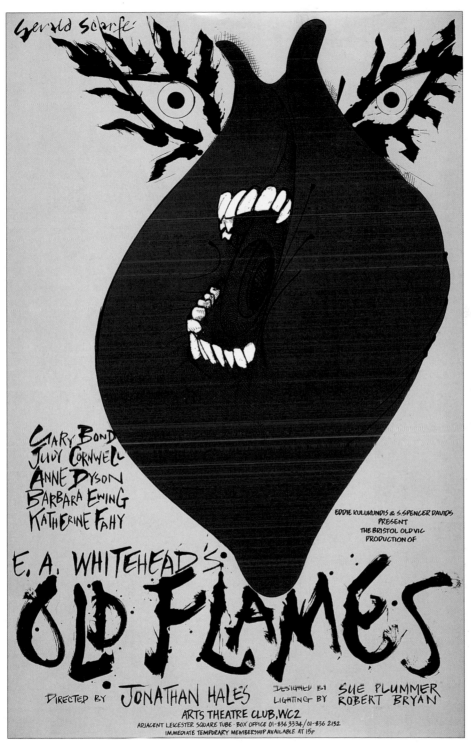

Poster design for *Old Flames*, Arts Theatre, 1975

Costume and set designs for *Get the Message* by Clive
King. Touring production, Molecule Theatre, 1987

MESSAGE
THE WILDERNESS

'WHAT THE BUTLER SAW'

Set and costume designs for *What the Butler Saw* by Joe
Orton, Oxford Playhouse, 1978

Design for one of six back projections for *No End of
Blame* by Howard Barker, Royal Court Theatre, 1981

Animation designs for Reg the Dog for Roger Waters' European and American tour, 1983

THE MERRY WIVES OF WINDSOR

The Queen Mother. One of a series of royal family
portraits designed as a backcloth for the Guthrie
Theatre, Minneapolis

Above: *Orpheus in the Underworld* by Offenbach,
English National Opera, London Coliseum, 1985.
Designs for the Can Can Girls' costumes

Right: Poster design for Michigan Opera Theatre, 1986

Overleaf: Act One: 'Thebes'. Backcloth design showing
Thebes as a respectable Victorian city

Following page: Act One: 'The Transformation'.
Backcloth showing what was going on behind closed
doors in Victorian Thebes. Houses swing round to
show their 'other sides'

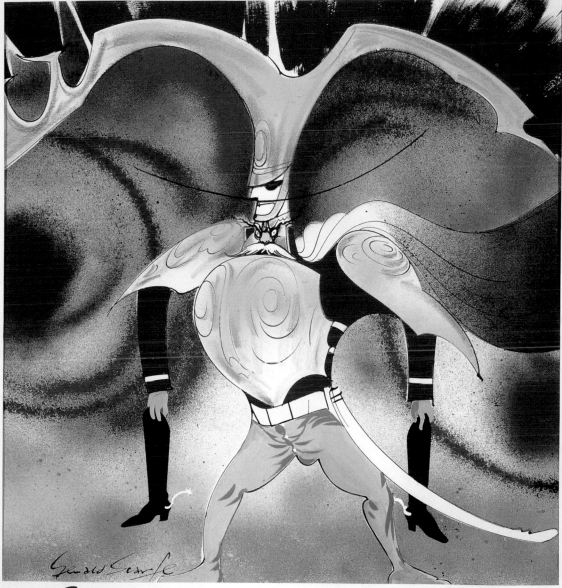

2. Fronts fly off to show interiors —
or 3. Fly in complete and begin buildings
or 4. Fly in additions to existing houses —
"ORPHEUS IN THE UNDERWORLD" ACT I S.

Honey

ACT I

Final figures much more caricature

Pop Seats.

Music

lecherous faces.

Costume designs for *Orpheus in the Underworld*

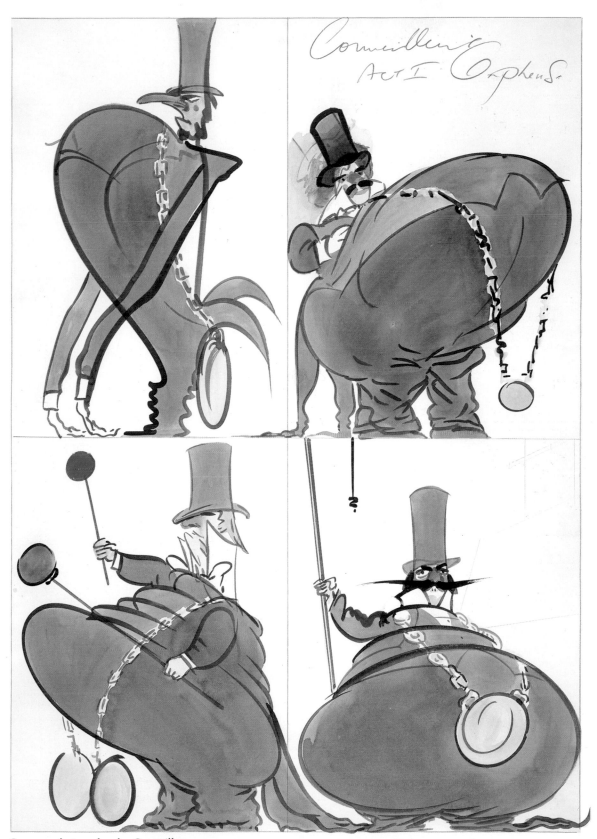

Costume designs for the Councillors

Left: Poster for Los Angeles Opera

Above: Jupiter is chided for his bizarre habit of disguising himself as an animal for his love trysts. English National Opera production, 1985

Below right: Pluto woos Eurydice, Los Angeles Opera production, 1987

Below left: Poster design for Houston Grand Opera, 1986

Hats w/ th plumes
Frock coats
Black ballet tights
Elastic sides boots

Tombstone to carry?

Dancing Undertakers.

Above left: Design for Mercury, the Gods' messenger

Above: Costume design for the Dancing Undertakers

Below left: Costume design for the Hounds of Hell

Overleaf: Jupiter is psychoanalysed for his old 'dressing up' problem

CASE NO 147

JUNE 15 CRETE

ANALYSIS

ACT II

metamorphosis

ALL IN WHITE COATS.
Other members don relevant masks?

Sepia?

Rondo.

Conch.

Projector and Scre

Swan.
Cock. El
Rhino
Coats

Frog. Penguin Skunk   STEAM
Snake. Zebra Chameleon
Lion Giraffe

morning Jupiter explode.

Costume design for the Roly Poly
Can Can Girls

Tulip

Spotted Dick and Custard

Pudding

Cauliflower 'Coli-flower'

Costume designs for a Tulip and Pluto's Lunch

Last act backcloth: The food in Heaven being so deadly
dull – nothing but ambrosia for breakfast, lunch and
dinner – the Gods descend to Hades for a jolly good
blow-out

Costume design for Eurydice

Laurence Olivier and
Kenneth Branagh as Henry V

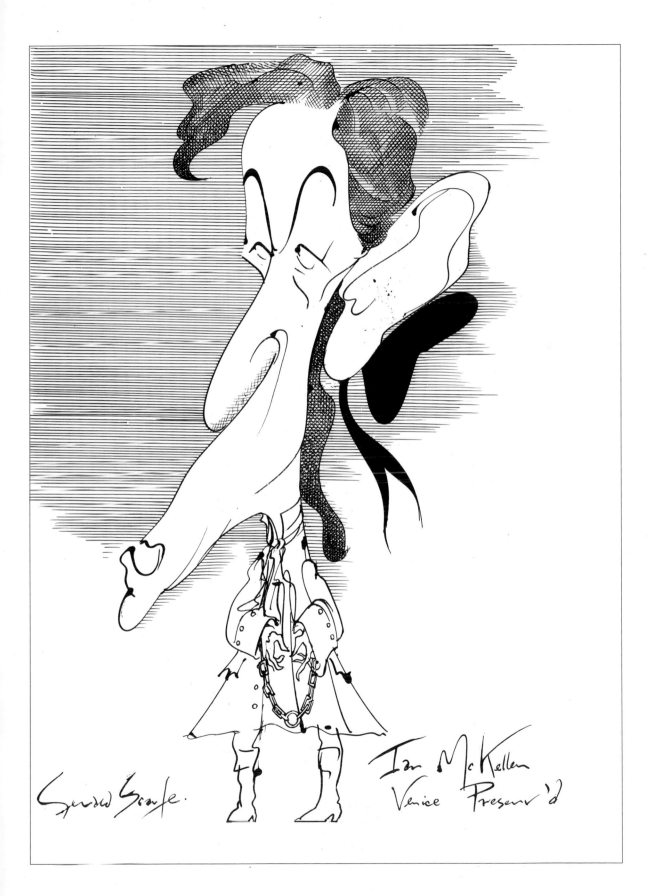

Gerald Scarfe.

Ian McKellen
Venice Preserv'd

MURRAY PERAHIA
IN REHEARSAL
FESTIVAL HALL
JUNE '86

Sir George Solti
Royal Festival Hall

Gerald Scarfe

Arturo Benedetti Michelangeli
Barbican June '86

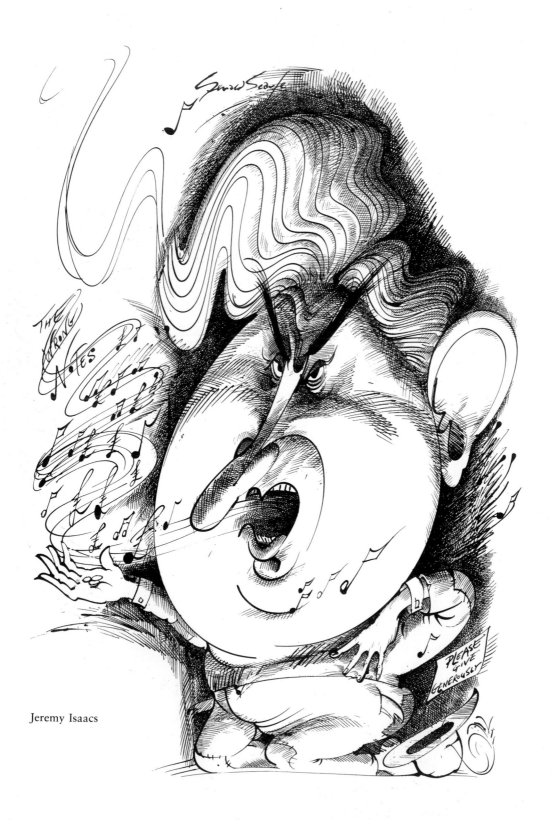

Jeremy Isaacs

THE NEW SLIM LINE
LUCIANO
Gerald Scarfe
SAVOY LONDON

Les Dawson

Woody Allen

CINDERELLA

FIRST COSTUME DESIGNS FOR TRIDENT + BARON HARDUP.

Designs for *Cinderella*, English National Opera, 1986

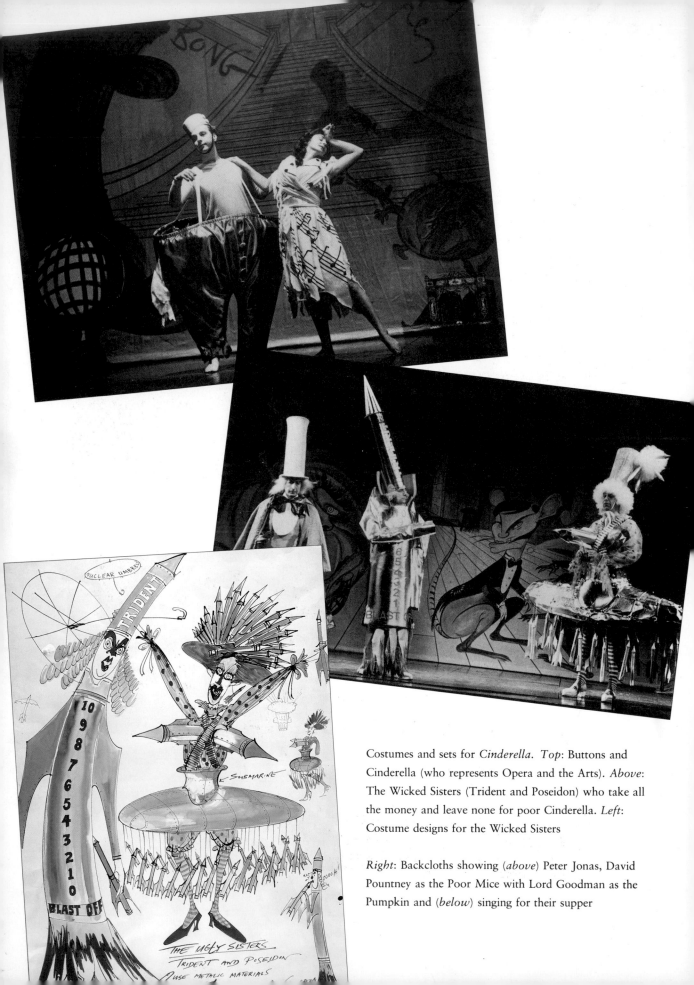

Costumes and sets for *Cinderella*. *Top*: Buttons and
Cinderella (who represents Opera and the Arts). *Above*:
The Wicked Sisters (Trident and Poseidon) who take all
the money and leave none for poor Cinderella. *Left*:
Costume designs for the Wicked Sisters

Right: Backcloths showing (*above*) Peter Jonas, David
Pountney as the Poor Mice with Lord Goodman as the
Pumpkin and (*below*) singing for their supper

'GREEK'

Backcloth for *Greek* by Stephen Berkoff, Wyndham's
Theatre, 1988

Right: Poster for exhibition at the Royal National
Theatre, 1987

THE SEVEN AGES OF MAN

AT FIRST THE INFANT MEWLING AND PUKING IN THE NURSES ARMS—

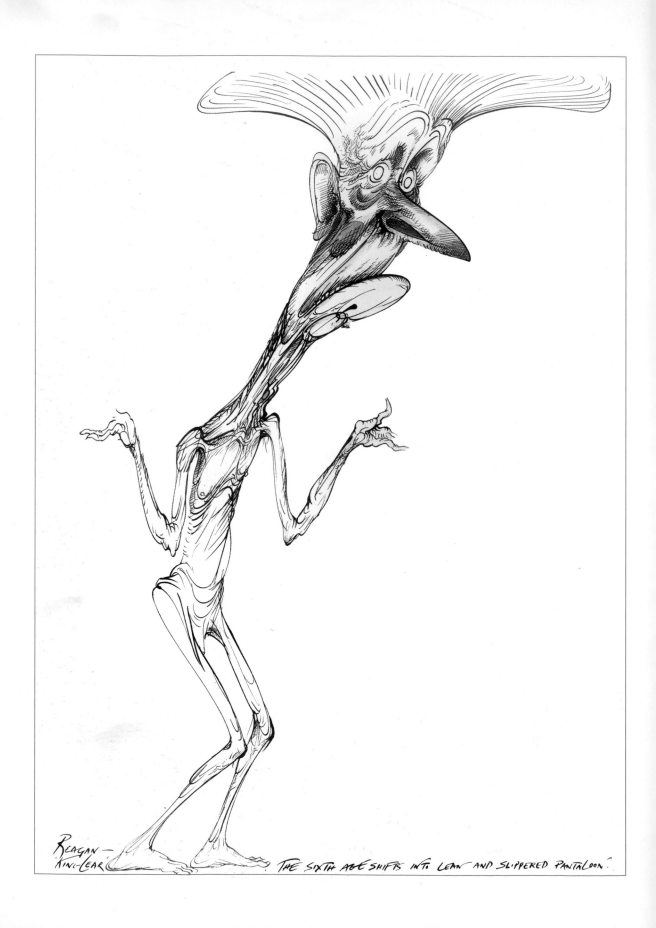

Reagan—
King-Lear

THE SIXTH AGE SHIFTS INTO LEAN AND SLIPPERED PANTALOON.

SCARFE BY SCARFE

Design and direction of *Scarfe by Scarfe*, *Arena*, BBC
TV, 1987. An autobiographical journey in which Gerald
Scarfe painted his life on the walls of a room

One of the designs for the titles of *Yes, Minister* and
Yes, Prime Minister, BBC TV

SCARFE'S FOLLIES

Design, production and direction of the film *Scarfe's Follies*, *Forty Minutes*, BBC TV, 1988

The Camel Folly designed and built during the programme

Above and right: Scenes from *Scarfe's Follies* showing
Terry Jones, Jane Asher, Bob Geldof and Ian McKellen

THE RAPTUROUSLY RHETORICAL NEIL KINNOCK

Costume design for *Ten Glorious Years*, a BBC TV
programme celebrating Mrs Thatcher's ten years in
office, 1989. Neil Kinnock as the Master of Ceremonies

Nigel Lawson as the Lord High Chancellor

Neil Kinnock, Nigel Lawson – the finished
costumes, *Ten Glorious Years*

Above: Model of Mrs Thatcher as Venus Rising from thc Waves amongst the Singing Policemen

Right: Mrs Thatcher and the Victorian Chorus

Overleaf: 'Royal Box' in the shape of Nigel Lawson

Rock and Roll

Madonna

Mick Jagger

Design, production and direction of *I Like the Girls Who Do ...*, a BBC TV film profile of Max Miller, 1989

Above: Backcloth for the film, showing Max Miller's home town, Brighton

Right: Poster for the film

Overleaf: Scenes from *I Like the Girls Who Do ...*

Designs for the inflatable Pig and Teacher. A live performance at the site of the demolished Berlin Wall

THE WALL — BERLIN '90

One of four caryatids designed for the Edinburgh Fringe shop front

Poster for the musical *Born Again*

Set design for the Shopping Mall and costume design for the Humanoid Rhino for *Born Again*, a musical based on Ionesco's *Rhinoceros*, Chichester Festival Theatre, 1990

Left: The Dancing Rhinos

Two rhinoceroses menace the shoppers in the Mall

Left: Mandy Patinkin as Martin dances with Daisy